THE ULTIMATE GUIDE TO AMONG US

Published in 2022 by Mortimer Children's Books Limited
An imprint of the Welbeck Publishing Group
Based in London and Sydney.
www.welbeckpublishing.com

All game information correct as of January 2022.

ISBN: 978 1 83935 179 2
Printed in Dongguan, China

1 3 5 7 9 10 8 6 4 2

Author: Kevin Pettman
Design: Rockjaw Creative
Design Manager: Matt Drew
Editorial Manager: Joff Brown
Production: Melanie Robertson

Picture Credit: Vidoslava/Shutterstock.com

THE ULTIMATE GUIDE TO AMONG US

HOW TO BE THE CLEVEREST CREWMATE ... OR THE DEADLIEST IMPOSTOR!

KEVIN PETTMAN

MORTIMER

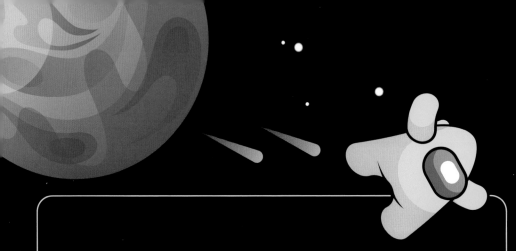

Who do you trust? Can you complete your tasks without being attacked? When will evil strike? All of these thoughts race through your mind as you explore the exciting adventures of Among Us!

This mobile, PC, and console game is packed with secret moves, sneaky decisions, sabotage, and some seriously "sus" characters. If you're picked as a Crewmate, the pressure is on to tackle tasks and sniff out the murderous player (or players!). Get given the Impostor role and it's time to be the bad guy and kill the Crew, but without being detected.

The Ultimate Guide to Among Us uncovers all you need to know to master every move and mission on your space-based journey. **READ ON ... IF YOU DARE!**

CONTENTS

CREWMATE GUIDE 16

IMPOSTOR Instructions 68

MYSTERY MISSION

Danger awaits in every room, corridor, and open space in Among Us. Choose your map and you will be assigned your role of Crewmate or Impostor. The Crew's mission is to complete tasks until the task bar is maxed out or work together to reveal who the Impostor—aka the mysterious murderer—is among you. The Impostor will conduct sabotage missions on the map and seek success by secretly killing all the Crew or getting innocent Crewmates ejected. It's a classic clash of good versus bad!

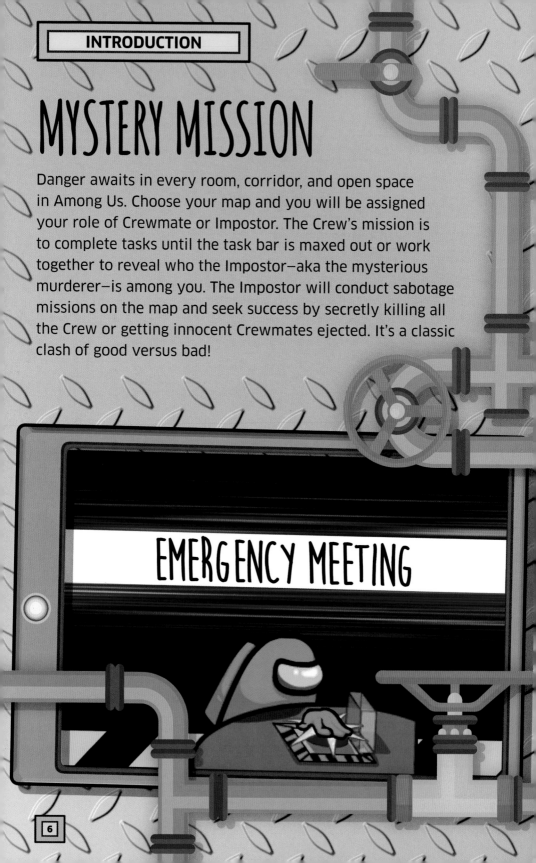

EMERGENCY MEETING

NASTY NUMBERS

Select the number of players you want in your game. The minimum is four and the upper limit is 15. With four players on screen there can be just one Impostor. Seven lets you set two Impostors, and to play with three Impostors you must have at least nine players involved. Having more Impostors changes the deadly dynamic of Among Us.

CLEVER CREW

As well as completing tasks the Crew can text chat to share who they think the Impostor could be. Text chat is possible in meetings, which happen after a dead body is reported or an emergency meeting is called. Impostors will also be part of the discussion.

COLOR CLASH

Players are referred to by the color of their suit. These include red, green, blue, pink, orange, and yellow.

SPACE TO STRIKE!

Everything may not be what it appears around the space, air, and intergalactic maps of Among Us. Impostors look just like regular Crewmates and nothing gives them away on the outside. Inside, though, these murderous characters are continually plotting to overpower the innocent players.

EVIL IDENTITY

So how can you spot the killer? Later you'll find much more info on deadly detection, but it's essential to scan the scene for key clues. Seeing a player enter a room and vanish through a vent (only Impostors can vent), faking tasks (only the Crew can do tasks), someone sticking close to a player to make a quick kill, and accusing lots of players in a meeting are all "dead" giveaways!

CHHHHHHH!

GHOST GAME

Crewmates and Impostors can become ghosts after being ejected or killed if the game continues. Ghost players are only seen by other ghosts and can't communicate with living players. They move through walls and Impostor ghosts may sabotage, although killing and venting are not possible.

ByeWorld29

VOTE TIME

When the chat's over after a dead body report or emergency meeting, it's time to vote. Every player, including the Impostor, can select a color to vote for—this is the person they think is the bad guy. There's also the opportunity to skip a vote if you are unsure who to select.

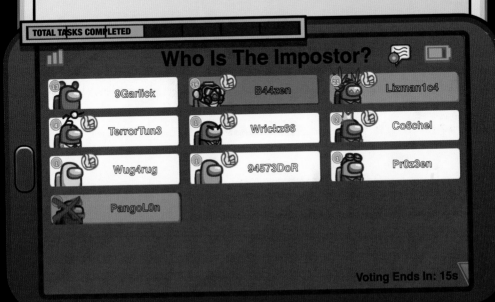

TOTAL TASKS COMPLETED

Who Is The Impostor?

13 9Garlick	16 B44zen	21 Lizman1c4
TerrorTun3	1 Wrickz66	2 Co6chel
1 Wug4rug	1 94573DoR	1 Pr0z3en
PangoL0n		

Voting Ends In: 15s

AWESOME UPDATES

InnerSloth, the Among Us developers, love to drop a deadly update and make this game even greater. Here are some of the major improvements they've made.

AIRSHIP MAP

The Among Us community went bonkers for the new Airship map! It was the fourth location added to the game and gives a whole new experience of tasks and sabotaging. Expect more maps as InnerSloth keeps us 100 percent entertained!

UNDERGROUND DEVELOPMENT

On the previous pages, you found out that only Impostors can use the underground vents ... although that's not strictly true following a 2021 update! The new Engineer role, which can be randomly given to a Crew member, allows an innocent player to vent.

ROLE PLAY

Scientist and Guardian Angel are two new roles for Crewmates. The Scientist has access to a portable vitals monitor to see the status of living and dead players, and the Guardian Angel is a ghost Crewmate who can cast a protective shield.

SHIFTING STRATEGY

Being able to "shapeshift" gives the Impostor a new angle of attack. This updated power lets the murderer take on the appearance of a living Crewmate—what a devilish disguise!

PLAYSTATION & XBOX

This is a biggie and brings console players into the world of Among Us. The game was open to PC, mobile, tablet, and Nintendo Switch players, but now the mighty machines of PlayStation and Xbox can get to grips with it.

COOL COSMICUBES

Cosmicubes is a new mechanic, with both free and paid-for options, to pick up cool cosmetics and gear for your Among Us character. Released at the end of 2021, it includes special pets, skins, hats, name plates, and visor cosmetics.

ACTIVE

MIRA COSMICUBE

0% Completed

VR-TASTIC

There are plans in place for a virtual reality (VR) version of Among Us, where The Skeld can be played in thrilling 3D!

STARS AND BEANS

Stars is a flashy new in-game premium currency that is paid for with real money. It opens the door to even more items and cosmicubes. Beans are a free resource dished out for regular online achievements and can be converted for new items.

GAME COMPLETE

② ▭▭▭▭▭▭ Lvl 3

x1.5
+100 x2.0
x2.5

0
Beans

TOP TIP

When it's not Halloween, picking up the themed hats may be possible by changing your device's date to an October date!

THEMED SCREAMS

Always check out the horrifying Halloween-themed adventures in October and early November. Some maps will be decorated with pumpkins, spiders, cobwebs, and slime, and there's the chance to wear spooky hats and visor cosmetics.

SMALL STUFF

Small and simple new additions to Among Us will add up to big changes to your gaming enjoyment. New 4K graphics, fresh suit colors such as tan, banana, rose and coral, mobile gaming support, and more robust servers are just some of the improvements.

DEADLY DIGITS

Check out some numbers you should know...

33

Among Us call their game updates "emergency meetings," which is cool. Emergency meeting 33 unveiled the major additions of four new roles, cosmicubes, a progression system, and more.

18

The fourth map, Airship, is the largest yet, with 18 rooms and 12 vents. Polus is just behind it with 17 rooms.

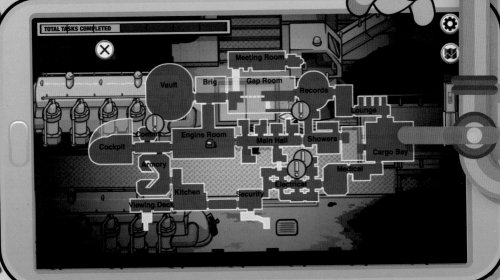

2020

This was the year when Among Us took over the gaming globe! The game was released in 2018, but two years later, it attracted tens of millions of users.

Custom Settings
Map: MIRA HQ
Impostors: 1
Confirm Ejects: On
Emergency Meetings: 3
Anonymous Votes: Off
Emergency Cooldown: 10s
Discussion Time: 15s
Voting Time: 15s
Player Speed: 1.25x
Crewmate Vision: 2.75x
Impostor Vision: 2.75x
Kill Cooldown: 20s
Kill Distance: Short
Task Bar Updates: Never
Visual Tasks: On
Common Tasks: 1
Long Tasks: 2
Short Tasks: 5

15

It used to be ten, but now you can have as many as 15 players involved in the same game. That's sooo many people to suspect!

15

The game celebrates its birthday every year (funnily enough!) on June 15. It was on this date that the extended 15-player lobby was announced.

2

There were rumors of Among Us 2 coming out, but instead it was ditched so the developers could focus on making the "OG" game even better. Smart move, folks.

CREWMATE GUIDE

It's time to learn the lethal lessons you need to keep the Impostor at bay, get your tasks done, and become an all-round clever Crewmate! This section takes a close-up look at the role of a Crew member and covers both the essentials and elite-level tactics to take you to victory. You're about to become a legend on every map, and get the tips and secrets needed to defeat the Impostor!

JOIN YOUR CREW

You will be a Crewmate more often than an Impostor, so make sure you can control the game and win all the secret battles.

TOTAL TASKS COMPLETED

FREE FOR ALL

New to the game? Get some training time under your spacesuit belt by selecting the freeplay mode and exploring a chosen map. You'll play against dummy characters and do tasks, visit rooms, and even use the vents if you switch to the Impostor role. Go to the laptop to choose tasks and role.

MAP MISSION

Continue using freeplay and familiarize your movements around each map. It can quickly become confusing to navigate rooms and corridors in a proper pressure-packed game. Tap the map button to get a display of all the rooms. Any with an exclamation mark show a task needing to be done there.

GO ONLINE

Choose the "online" mode from the start screen to be given three choices: host, public, and private. Host means you can create your own game with your preferred settings, public lets you join an open game, or you can enter a friend's private game if they share a six-letter code with you.

RerkzD2

No12Zap

SOLO STYLE

Freeplay mode is the only single-player option. In this mode, the other Crew are NPC (non-playable character) figures controlled by the computer.

SETTING OFF

Select the settings you want before beginning your battle in space. Having knowledge of game types and controls will create the perfect out-of-this-world atmosphere for your Crewmate contests.

DEFAULT DETAILS

Of course you don't have to inspect the Among Us pre-game settings. You can just launch off with the defaults in place! This is often what you'll do as a fresh-faced new Crewmate on the scene. After a while, though, you'll notice that adjusting the settings delivers a game that suits your style and preference.

— ☐ ✕

TAKE CONTROL

From the settings icon, you can tailor your move and control preferences. Mobile and tablet players can toggle between touch and joystick movement, while PC users have the option to control through keyboard or keyboard with mouse. Try different settings in freeplay before confirming your favorite.

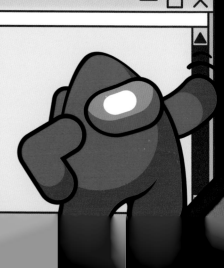

SOUND DECISION

Decide on your SFX and music levels. Having both set to maximum could be a no-brainer for you, but dropping music down and leaving SFX at full may just enhance your all-around enjoyment... and boost the scary sounds you really want to be listening out for.

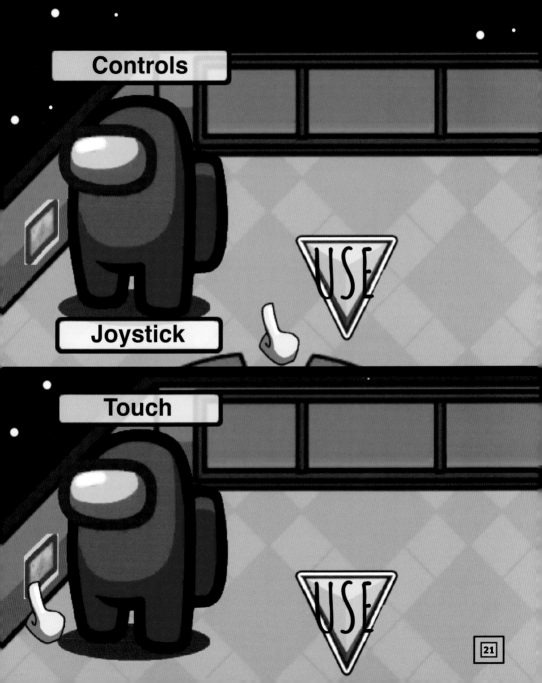

Controls

Joystick

Touch

GAME STYLE

As a game host, there are lots of game settings to configure as you create a fun (and frightening!) scene for your Crewmate colleagues.

LONG, LETHAL LIST

From kill distance to cooldown times, confirm ejects, player speed, player vision, and task bar displays, take time to study and master what each preference can offer. As a general rule, placing the most important settings to **discussion time 30s, voting time 45s, player speed 1.25x, Crewmate vision 1.75x, and Impostor vision 2x** should make for a lively but manageable battle.

CUSTOM SETTINGS

	Recommended Settings		
# Impostors	⊖	2	✚
Confirm Ejects		✔	
# Emergency Meetings	⊖	1	✚
Emergency Cooldown	⊖	20s	✚
Discussion Time	⊖	30s	✚
Voting Time	⊖	45s	✚
Anonymous Votes		☐	

MIX AND MATCH

These settings are examples of the type of Among Us game you can create as host...

Game: Beginner

Opt for two or three emergency meetings, player speed of 1x, discussion and voting times of around 60 seconds, and similar settings for both cooldowns.

Game: Intermediate

Reduce discussion and voting time to 30 seconds to make people think quicker. Have more than one Impostor, to give players a double threat.

Game: Advanced

Set player speed to 2.25x to help cover the map, keep emergency cooldown at 20s, and a long kill distance to give the Impostor a bigger strike range.

Game: Elite

Switch anonymous votes off to ramp up the tension, give the Impostor a greater vision boost, have two emergency meetings and a very quick voting time to really deal out the drama!

TEN TOP TIPS

Before you take a close-up look at the maps, take in these quick general tips to help you get the upper hand on the Impostor.

1 BUDDY UP

If you can, try to team up with another innocent Crewmate early on. Do some tasks together as a pair, move around with close proximity, and get the trust of each other before a vote.

6/8

2 SAFETY IN NUMBERS

Whether in the early, mid, or late game, keeping the Crewmates close can be very frustrating for the Impostors. It means there are witnesses and few opportunities to make a kill.

3 CRITICAL CALL

Dealing with a critical sabotage is, well, critical! When the screen flashes red and the alert sounds out, get it dealt with ASAP otherwise the Impostor will grab victory!

Office   Admin

Reactor

Laboratory

Decontamination

Launchpad   Locker Room   Communications   Storage   Cafeteria

MedBay

Balcony

MedBay

4 SEE SENSE

The Impostor's vision needs to be slightly greater than the Crewmates' setting. This gives the Impostor a slight advantage in electrical lights-out sabotages, and is needed for fair play between the two groups.

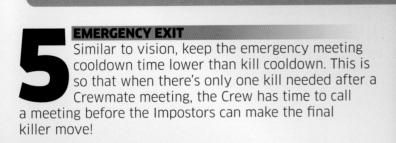

Custom Settings
Map: The Skeld
Impostors: 1 (Limit:0)
Confirm Ejects: On
Emergency Meetings: 1
Anonymous Votes: Off
Emergency Cooldown: 15s
Discussion Time: 15s
Voting Time: 120s
Player Speed: 1x
Crewmate Vision: 1x
Impostor Vision: 1.5x
Kill Cooldown: 45s
Kill Distance: Medium
Task Bar Updates: Always
Visual Tasks: On
Common Tasks: 1
Long Tasks: 1
Short Tasks: 2
Scientist: 0 with 0% Chance
Guardian Angel: 0 with 0% Chance
Engineer: 0 with 0% Chance
Shapeshifter: 0 with 0% Chance

Jerb7n

5 EMERGENCY EXIT

Similar to vision, keep the emergency meeting cooldown time lower than kill cooldown. This is so that when there's only one kill needed after a Crewmate meeting, the Crew has time to call a meeting before the Impostors can make the final killer move!

Custom Settings
Map: The Skeld
Impostors: 1 (Limit:0)
Confirm Ejects: On
Emergency Meetings: 1
Anonymous Votes: Off
Emergency Cooldown: 15s
Discussion Time: 15s
Voting Time: 120s
Player Speed: 1x
Crewmate Vision: 1x
Impostor Vision: 1.5x
Kill Cooldown: 45s
Kill Distance: Medium
Task Bar Updates: Always
Visual Tasks: On
Commomn Tasks: 1
Long Tasks: 1
Short Tasks: 2
Scientist: 0 with 0% Chance
Guardian Angel: 0 with 0% Chance
Engineer: 0 with 0% Chance
Shapeshifter: 0 with 0% Chance

6GullSevn

6 TOUGH TASK

Keep the task bar set to "always." This means both Crew and Impostors can monitor the overall progress of the game's tasks. Putting it to "never" makes the goal of both roles insanely tough to gauge!

7 WISE MOVES

If you are new to a map, or to Among Us in general, then moving through the map in a clockwise or counterclockwise path could help you keep track of where you are and not get lost. This is not always possible, but could be a handy tactic while in freeplay mode, for example.

Gwar5h

8

SAY WHAT?

For players under 13, there is the quickchat feature to use for communicating during meetings. Added in 2021, it has seven functions of accusation, Crew, systems, location, statements, question and response.

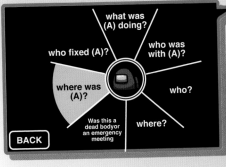

9

LANGUAGE LESSON

If you have text chat, or when talking about Among Us with friends, there are slang words and phrases you will probably need to know. **Sus (suspect or suspicious), cams (cameras), stack (large group kill),** and **out (outside of a location)** are some you may come across.

10

KICK OFF

From the lobby, the game host has the power to kick out or ban a player if they misbehave or are AFK (away from keyboard) for long periods. Accessed by the boot icon, it is a simple way to keep other players happy in the games.

MAPS: THE AIRSHIP

Take a tour around the biggest Among Us map to understand the ins and outs of this giant flying fortress.

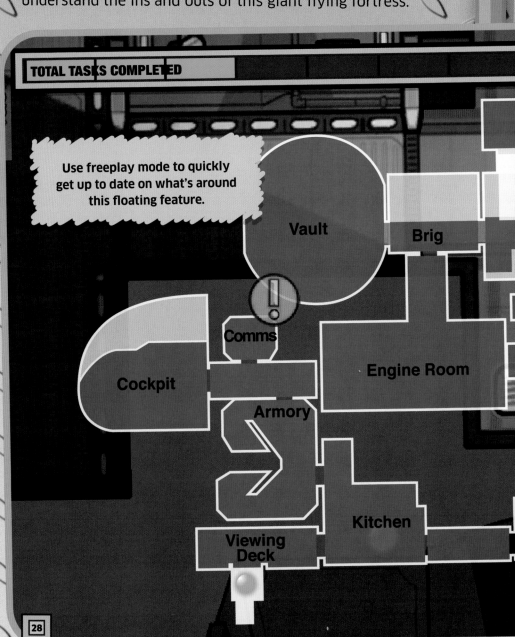

TOTAL TASKS COMPLETED

Use freeplay mode to quickly get up to date on what's around this floating feature.

Vault

Brig

Comms

Cockpit

Engine Room

Armory

Kitchen

Viewing Deck

The northerly Meeting room may appear isolated and a spot where the Impostor could kill, but it's fairly safe and busy with three tasks. Emergency meeting button is here.

Security has cameras where you can track other players' movements around The Airship. Sneaky!

Small groups of players, such as seven or fewer, may struggle around The Airship as the Impostor has lots of space to surprise.

Entrance to the outside area can be gained through Security and Viewing deck.

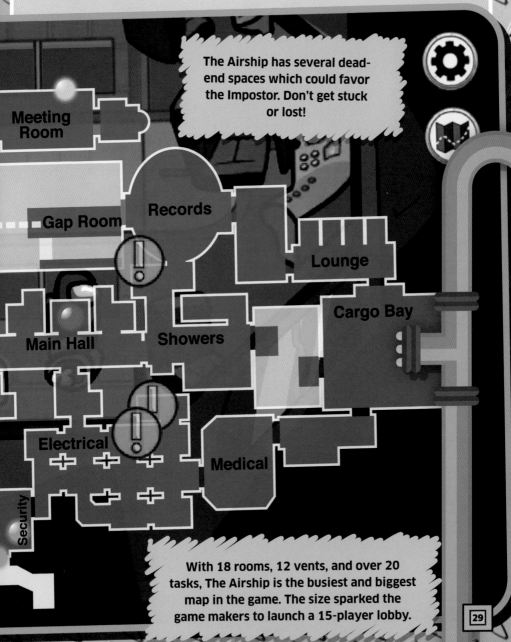

The Airship has several dead-end spaces which could favor the Impostor. Don't get stuck or lost!

Meeting Room

Gap Room

Records

Lounge

Cargo Bay

Main Hall

Showers

Electrical

Medical

Security

With 18 rooms, 12 vents, and over 20 tasks, The Airship is the busiest and biggest map in the game. The size sparked the game makers to launch a 15-player lobby.

ROOM REQUEST

When you load up The Airship you are presented with the choice of starting in one of three random rooms. This is a unique feature to this map. Pick the room you think will give you the best start, or the one you feel most comfortable spawning inside.

Brig   **Records**   **Cargo Bay**

Time remaining: 9

LADDER TIME

The Airship is the first map to have different levels and use ladders to move. They are found in the Meeting room and Gap room, and connecting the Main Hall with Electrical. Ladders can be climbed and slid down, which is great fun, and players will hear you when you are on one.

RECORDS

Prizzm

Gap Room

VENT SYSTEM

While The Airship is vast, the venting system it has is much more compact. There are four clusters to be aware of. The Vault is connected to Viewing Deck, via Cockpit, as a useful north-south route for the Impostor and Engineer. The Kitchen and Engine are linked underground, and so too is the Gap room to Main Hall. Records-Showers-Cargo bay is the final vent link. Get to know where they are, both from a good and evil team perspective.

Nert5nU

PAUSE PLAY

If an Impostor uses a ladder, their kill cooldown time is paused. Impostors also can't sabotage while on a ladder.

NEW TASKS

Of course, with a new map comes new jobs to do!
A memorable mission for the Crew includes having to clean
the toilets in Lounge, where the highlighted toilet must be
plunged. Eww! Picking up the scattered towels, and fixing the
showers in Showers, over to the east side of the Airship, are
two more bathroom-based tasks.

NO VIS

Upon its release, The Airship did not
have any visual tasks to complete,
unlike the first three maps. You may
think it has visuals, but even collecting
towels and cleaning toilets are not
technically visuals: a visual task gives
a display to others that the mission is
actually in progress.

GOOD CONNECTION

The Cockpit has two short tasks
and one short and long task,
which is to upload data. To finish
upload data, your mobile device
must be taken outside for a
good connection.

MOVE ALONG

As well as ladders, the moving platform in the Gap Room is another example of a motion device released with The Airship map. Standing on the platform moves you across the gap. Only one person can use it at a time, and you can't summon it to you if you're on the opposite side to it.

Gap Room

Gap Room

SPARKS FLYING

Be on full alert if you enter Electrical, which is wedged between Security and Medical. It can become a dark maze of a room with plenty of spots to get lost or trapped. Use the ladder for a speedy exit if you're caught.

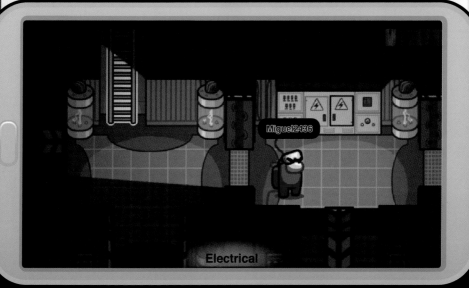

Electrical

MAPS: THE SKELD

Still the most visited map in Among Us, it's time to travel through your guide to The Skeld.

Because of its quite compact layout, it can be fairly easy for new players to get familiar with The Skeld's routes, hallways, and task locations.

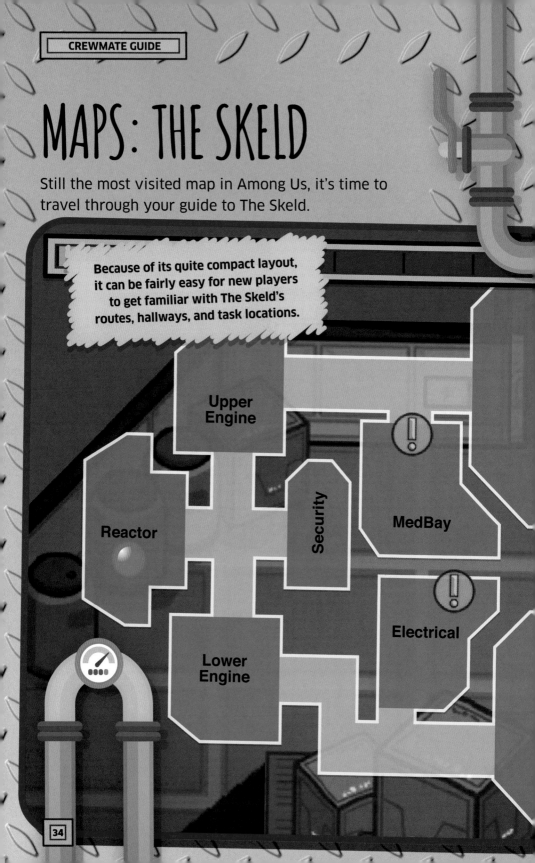

Upper Engine

Reactor

Security

MedBay

Lower Engine

Electrical

Players spawn in the Cafeteria, which is a large room ideally located in a central area. This is also the spot of the emergency meeting button.

The size of Cafeteria and Storage means they act like a natural east-west break and almost divide The Skeld into two sections.

The two vents in Reactor are quite easy to notice – they're not hidden in corners or behind machinery and furniture.

The Skeld is the third largest arena. It has 14 main locations to explore.

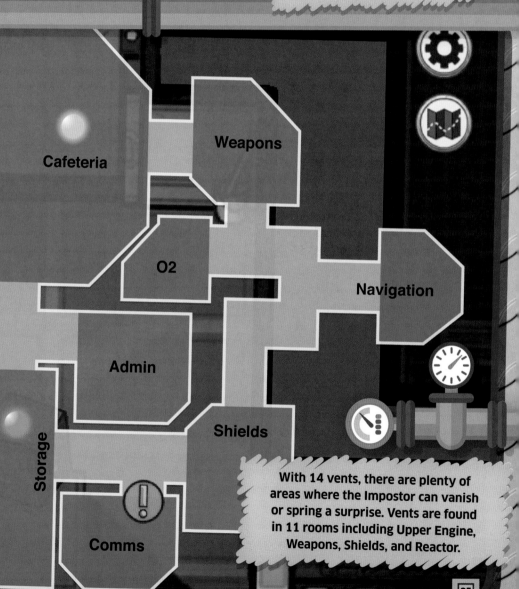

Cafeteria

Weapons

O2

Navigation

Admin

Storage

Shields

Comms

With 14 vents, there are plenty of areas where the Impostor can vanish or spring a surprise. Vents are found in 11 rooms including Upper Engine, Weapons, Shields, and Reactor.

SECURE STATUS

Security room has cameras that spy on some prime spots around The Skeld map. Scan the screen and check out what's happening in the areas between Security and Reactor, outside MedBay, to the north of Storage, and between O2 and Navigation.

RED WARNING

When the cameras are being monitored, it triggers the red warning light on each of them. Keep an eye on the four cameras for when they start to emit the tiny flash.

TOTAL TASKS COMPLETED

M1zz1nT

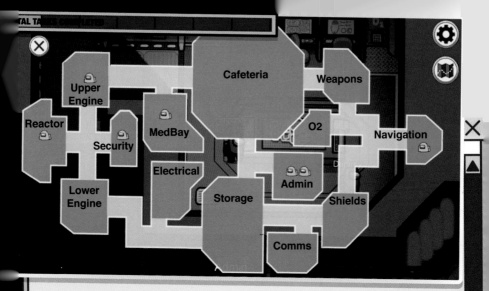

AWESOME ADMIN

Click the map in Admin on The Skeld and you can see a map of where all players currently are. It doesn't pick up suit colors and there may be a slight lag in showing exact player locations, but it's still ultra-handy in showing all Crew and Impostor whereabouts.

OPEN TUNNEL

The vent between O2 and Navigation is out in the open, located in the hallway. This is also an area covered by security cameras, so it's a risky move for Impostors to vent here, unlike the other room-based vents which are more protected. Crew can cover cams to see what goes on here.

MAPS: MIRA HQ

This is the business center for the space company MIRA.
Head there now for this speedy dash around the map!

TOTAL TASKS COMPLETED

MIRA HQ is found high up in the atmosphere, with a dramatic feel that suits its dark position in the Among Us galaxy. It was added to the game a year after The Skeld.

With just 12 rooms and less hallways and corridors, most of the action and events take place in rooms. Be prepared whenever you step inside one!

Reactor

Decontamination

Launchpad

Because of the tight space, MIRA HQ is best left to more experienced players who can think, move, and communicate quickly when needed!

Running north-south, the dangerous Decontamination area is a channel where doors lock at each end for a short while once you enter.

Hunt for the emergency meeting button in Cafeteria if you're suddenly desperate to call the Crewmates together for discussion.

Use the helpful door log system to check a player's movements.

Greenhouse

Office

Admin

Laboratory

Unlike The Skeld, the corridors are quite long and uncluttered, offering improved lines of vision for Crew and Impostors.

Locker Room

Comms

Storage

Cafeteria

MedBay

Balcony

LINK UP

All of the vast network of vents around MIRA HQ are connected, meaning there's an underground passage for the Impostor to just about anywhere. The only rooms that do not have access to a vent are Locker Room, Communications, Storage, and Cafeteria.

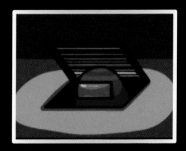

CAMERA SHY

MIRA HQ is not covered by an army of CCTV cameras picking up player movements—in fact there are zero cams! This is another reason why it's a tough map for Crewmates to crack. Impostors can get ahead of the game by staying out of sight.

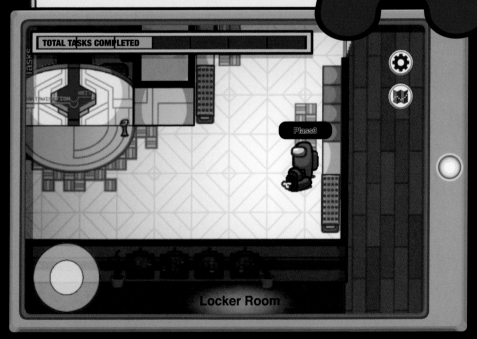

TOTAL TASKS COMPLETED

Plass3

Locker Room

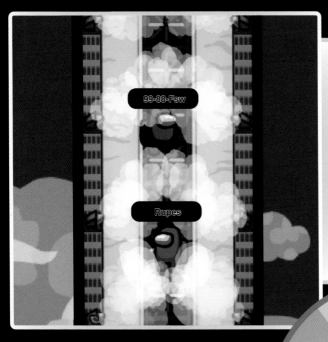

DEADLY DECON

The Decontamination corridor is only for brave Crew to enter, particularly with just one other player who may turn out to be an Impostor. When the doors lock and gas fills the room there's no chance to escape if a killer move is made.

SPACE WORK

Staff at MIRA HQ are said to be conducting research, data collection, and exploration around high-level outer space studies!

TRACK BACK

Again, as a Crewmate don't forget to use the Admin ability in the Admin room up in the north of MIRA HQ. It can be a trek to get there, but the effort is worth it as being able to track the location of the other players is very helpful, especially with no cameras to view.

MAPS: POLUS

Keep your eyes peeled and know the route to take to call an emergency meeting, in this frightening and freezing map.

TOTAL TASKS COMPLETED

Vents near to Electrical, Laboratory, and Office are visible to the cameras. Crew can catch the murderers this way.

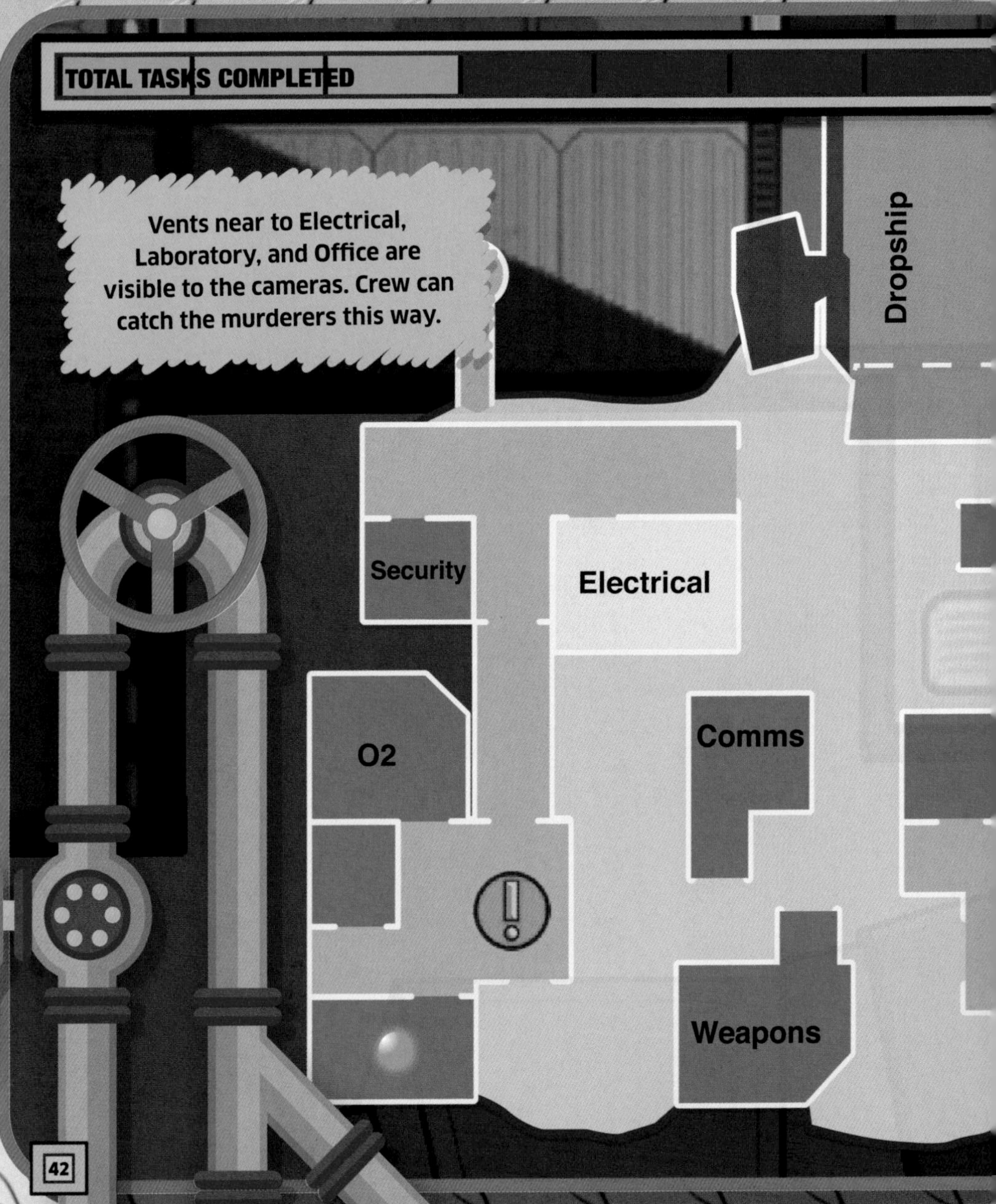

Dropship

Security

Electrical

O2

Comms

Weapons

Polus has two Decontamination departments, found near to Admin and Laboratory. This spells double trouble because the few seconds spent trapped here could mean it's game over!

As a general rule, the south side of Polus is often safer due to there

being less vents and more distance from the Dropship spawn area.

Fan of the great outdoors? There's plenty out in the open space of Polus—just wrap up warm in this f-f-f-freezing landscape!

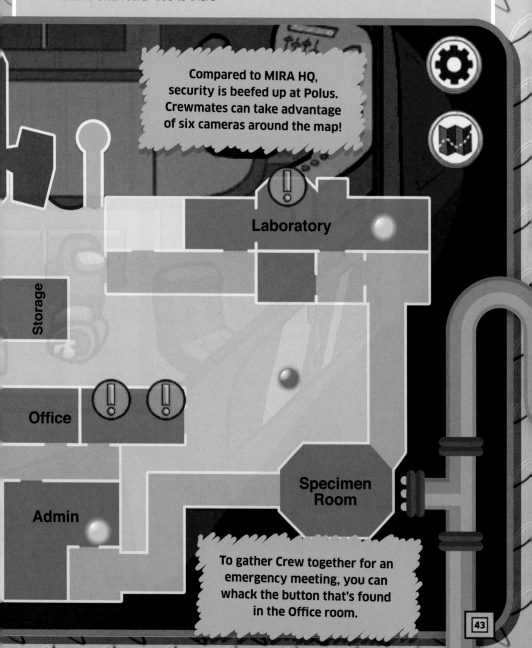

Compared to MIRA HQ, security is beefed up at Polus. Crewmates can take advantage of six cameras around the map!

Laboratory

Storage

Office

Specimen Room

Admin

To gather Crew together for an emergency meeting, you can whack the button that's found in the Office room.

HIGH NUMBERS

Games at Polus with not many players involved are often tense and tricky. With less Crew players on this base, catching the Impostor is tough unless you're an advanced-level gamer. Games with 15 involved can be great fun here, though.

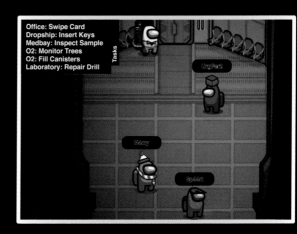

Office: Swipe Card
Dropship: Insert Keys
Medbay: Inspect Sample
O2: Monitor Trees
O2: Fill Canisters
Laboratory: Repair Drill

Tasks

VITAL ACTION

Head to the Office to use an important tool in your quest as a Crewmate. The vitals signs machine displays player status. It will show green for an active player, gray for a death in a previous round, and red to depict a kill since the last meeting.

ONE TO WATCH

You've heard about the good security camera coverage at Polus, but there's a downside as well. Only one camera can be viewed on the screen at a time, so keep flicking between the cams in order to see anything sus taking place.

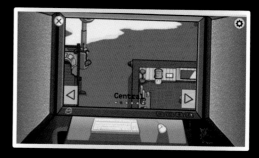

DROP OUT

The Dropship has two Crewmate tasks—insert keys and chart course—which are often done in the early game, meaning Crew may not return here very often. Be very careful if another player wants to lead you here, as it may be the Impostor trying to isolate you!

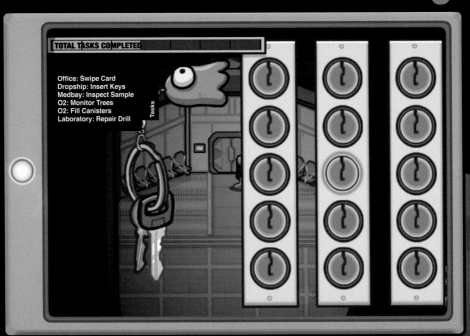

TOTAL TASKS COMPLETED

Office: Swipe Card
Dropship: Insert Keys
Medbay: Inspect Sample
O2: Monitor Trees
O2: Fill Canisters
Laboratory: Repair Drill

Tasks

TASK TIME

Doing tasks and loading up the task bar is a crucial part of Among Us. Crew can do a range of tasks around the maps, but Impostors can only do fake tasks.

CREWMATE PROGRESS

The green task bar at the top of your screen will begin to fill up when the Crew's jobs have been completed. This is key to getting victory over the Impostor. The task bar can be seen by both Crew and Impostors, unless it is switched to "never" in settings. There are four types of tasks—short, long, common, and visual—and the number of the first three in this list can be altered. You need to be the host of a game though. Through 'customize settings', the maximum number of short tasks can be set to five, with three for long and two for common.

SHORT TASK: A short task requires just a single action, and these are quick and easy to do.
Example: Buy beverage on MIRA HQ
Number to do: 40+

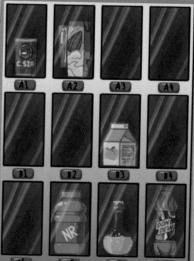

LONG TASK: More time-consuming and will demand multiple stage tasks, moving locations, and even waiting.
Example: Develop photos on The Airship
Number to do: 25+

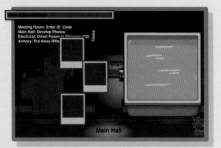

COMMON TASK: Dished out to all Crewmates and must be completed by every Crew member.
Example: Enter ID code on The Airship and MIRA HQ
Number to do: 10+

VISUAL TASK: These show an action or animation on screen while being done.
Example: Submit scan on The Skeld, Polus, and MIRA HQ
Number to do: 7+

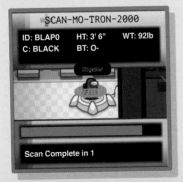

SCAN-MO-TRON-2000
ID: BLAP0   HT: 3' 6"   WT: 92lb
C: BLACK   BT: O-

Scan Complete in 1

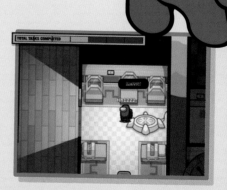

TASK TACTICS

Take your task gameplay to another level with these top tactics, tips, and hints for when you're busy doing a mission.

CLEANING UP

Shortly after the fourth Airship map, a new task arrived that had Crewmates smiling from ear to ear inside their visors! Called 'clean vent', when Crew have this task they can clean the Impostor's evil underground escapes which will prevent them from using them. This can be used on the Airship, MIRA HQ, and The Skeld maps.

Ventricce5

Weapons

PIZZA PARTY

When cleaning a vent, objects like old pizza slices, a tennis ball, and hairclip are removed. Impostors can still operate in vents, but not the specific one that is currently being cleaned. What's mega helpful is that if a murderer is already inside the vent when it starts to be cleaned, the task will chuck that player out. You'll catch the Impostor in an instant!

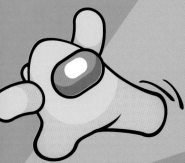

MAIN MISSIONS

The Airship's Main Hall is a long corridor with six small spaces leading from it. The Main Hall can have as many as five tasks, so expect it to be a busy area for Crew and Impostors because of this, and also as it's in a central location. Divert power, develop photos, decontaminate, fix wiring, and empty garbage range in mission types to short, long, and common.

TOTAL TASKS COMPLETED

Destroyed: 5

BATHROOM BONUS

The Showers room, directly east of Main Hall, can also have five tasks. This is a busy location!

VISUAL CLUES

Listen up Crewmates—the importance of doing visual tasks can't be stressed enough! Doing one of these jobs, such as submit scan on the first three maps and clear asteroids on Polus and The Skeld, gives a visual indicator and rubberstamps that you are not an Impostor.

CHANGING TASKS

Be mindful that not all types of tasks are the same on each map. For example, the fuel engines mission is a long task on The Airship, The Skeld, and Polus but just a short task on MIRA HQ. Make sure you know the time and effort it takes to do the same task on different locations, and don't get caught out!

REFUEL STATION

Seeb0ldr

DEAD SERIOUS

When Crewmates are killed or ejected, they become Ghosts. Ghosts can still do tasks and help the living Crew folk reach their task target. Ghosts have excellent vision that's not buffed by walls, and move at a slightly faster rate than regular Crewmates. They can also communicate with other murdered members.

TASK RECALL

If you have a good memory and remember your tasks, then tap the task tab to slide it to the side of your screen. Tap it again to recall it.

ROLE WITH IT

Tour through the three new Crewmate roles and discover how they can be a gamechanger in the hunt to defeat the enemy!

ENGINEER

The Engineer's super power is being able to vent, just like the Impostor! This can give the Crew a gain over the enemy, as the engineer ducks through tunnels to track the murderer. Use the 'host options' section to set how long the Engineer can spend underground, the vent cooldown time, and probability of the role coming up. If you're new to this role, then use free play mode to brain up on it.

Don't spend too long in vents, as the Crew may think you're the Impostor!

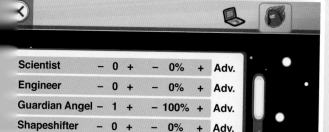

Scientist	– 0 +	– 0% +	Adv.
Engineer	– 0 +	– 0% +	Adv.
Guardian Angel	– 1 +	– 100% +	Adv.
Shapeshifter	– 0 +	– 0% +	Adv.

4EvaDSA

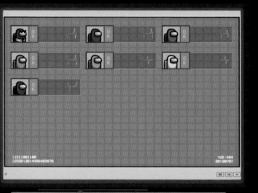

SCIENTIST

The clever Scientist has a fancy tool to take on the Impostors. Their portable vitals monitor gives them access to check on the status of all Crew in the game from anywhere on the map. They can see if players are dead or alive and watching their screen could make them the first to report a strike. The portable vitals is different than the stationary device.

The vitals machine will drain its battery but when the Scientist does tasks it is recharged!

GUARDIAN ANGEL

Think of the Guardian Angel role as a heavenly security officer. If the probability of this role is set to 100 percent, then the first Crewmate to die will take on the job. Guardian Angel is a ghost that has the power to throw a protective shield around a Crew member so the Impostor can't kill them. It's a smart Crew tactic, and the murderer's malicious move won't register.

Guardian Angel can be set to visible so that the Impostor is able to see the protect shield in use!

GUARDIAN ANGEL

Myrobia

CREWMATE CHAT

When you meet up with your Crew after an emergency meeting has been called, you need to know what to say ... or not what to say!

TALK SMART
Always, always think about what you say during a discussion. You have to get your thoughts out quickly, but never say stuff just for the sake of it. That could look sus.

WORD COUNT
Don't say too much as a Crewmate in a meeting. Other players could think you're trying to cover your back as the Impostor, and vote for you in the next round.

SPEAK UP
That said, gamers who say nothing or very little could attract unwanted attention from your fellow Crew! Always have an opinion, even if it's a brief one.

VISUAL VERIFICATION
If you saw a Crewmate doing a visual task, then you know they are to be trusted and you can tell the rest of your gang.

SHARE STUFF

If you actually witnessed something that incriminates the Impostor, like venting or a killing, then say so to the group.

WHEREABOUTS

Tell players where you were when the meeting or body report was made. There's a chance other Crew can verify it, and you'll then have a clear story.

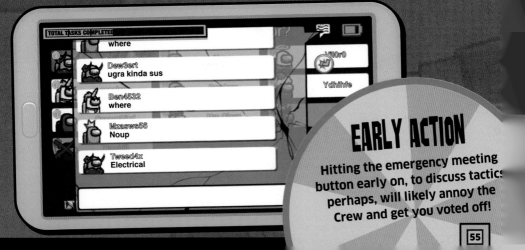

EARLY ACTION

Hitting the emergency meeting button early on, to discuss tactics perhaps, will likely annoy the Crew and get you voted off!

VOTING STRATEGY

As long as anonymous voting is set to off, after a discussion you can then see who votes for who as the Impostor.

DEADLY DECISION

If you made a case for a particular Crewmate in discussion and then voted another way, that looks very suspect and players could find you hard to trust.

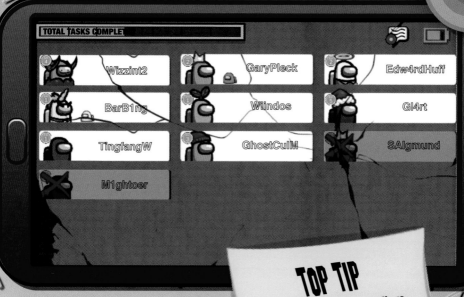

QUICK VOTE

Look out for a player who makes a very early vote. Without taking time to decide, is this the Impostor targeting an innocent Crewmate and trying to build up a backing and secure their own passage?

TOP TIP

There's a green confirm button once you do vote, just in case you tap or click on a player you don't want to vote for.

FRIENDLY VOTE

If you have been playing with another Crewmate, doing tasks together and moving around the map as a pair, then voting for them as your in-game pal makes total sense.

SKIP THROUGH

There's nothing wrong with skipping a vote if you can't decide who to choose and don't want to call out an innocent, but it's best not to do this more than once. You'll look weak and suspicious.

GUT FEELING

Much of the time this is all you have to rely on! You may just get a feeling that a person is very sus and deserves to get your vote. It's not nice, but often gets results in Among Us.

ID THE IMPOSTOR: 10 TIPS

Don't ignore these simple ways to single out the Impostor!

1 Someone popping up around the map quickly, but not seen often, could be using vents.

2 If a player makes a strong case for an Impostor but the other Crew don't act, then that person could be next on the killer's hitlist. Remember meeting conversations.

3 Look out for a player who seems to avoid cameras– that's often a good sign of their guilt.

4 Someone standing still and not having much of a plan. Genuine Crewmates will be busy doing tasks.

5 If a player never calls an emergency meeting, then they could be avoiding difficult discussions.

6 Someone who is spotted walking away from a dead body. Duh!

7 Seeing a player repeating a task is always ultra shady. If they are genuine, then that task will have been done the first time.

8 Someone seen tailing a Crewmate looking for a kill, but perhaps then scared away by others appearing.

9 Standing near vents. The Impostor could be waiting to dive down once the coast is clear.

10 Crewmates don't need to lie, but Impostors do it all the time! If you can verify what a person says is nonsense, you've cracked it!

SPOTTING THE SUSPECT: TRICKS & TECHNIQUES

The best ways for Crewmates to single out and identify the Impostor. These tips will make you a very valuable team player.

SHAPESHIFTER DOUBLE

Shapeshifting is a new Impostor role explained on pages 74-75. Essentially, if a Crewmate sees two of the same player together in the same place, or heavily suspects two identical players are both on the map, then one of them is an Impostor!

DOOR DETAILS

Impostors love to door sabotage and lock players in a room. If, for example, you know two players are in Upper Engine on The Skeld, but the door locks and a kill is made with the vent then being used, you know the escaped player did the deed.

SCARY SELFIE

As we say on page 44, watching vitals in the Office of Polus can sometimes really pay off. If a Crewmate is watching it and a player suddenly goes red, meaning they've died, and the body is reported immediately, then chances are it's a self-report and you can nab the reporter!

DID YOU KNOW?

A self-report is when the Impostor actually calls in the body they just killed as a way to take suspicion away from their own evil action.

DEAD BODY REPORTED

ENGINEER ADVICE

On MIRA HQ, the vents are all connected. If you are Crew with the new Engineer role, you can jump through the vents and pop up in lots of rooms looking to potentially spot the Impostor making a kill.

SCIENCE LESSON

As a Scientist Crewmate, try to keep your visor eyes focused on who is moving with who and which players appear to be working together. Using vitals, if one of that pair then dies then the other could be the prime suspect. This takes practice to perfect, but is very helpful when discussing with your Crew members.

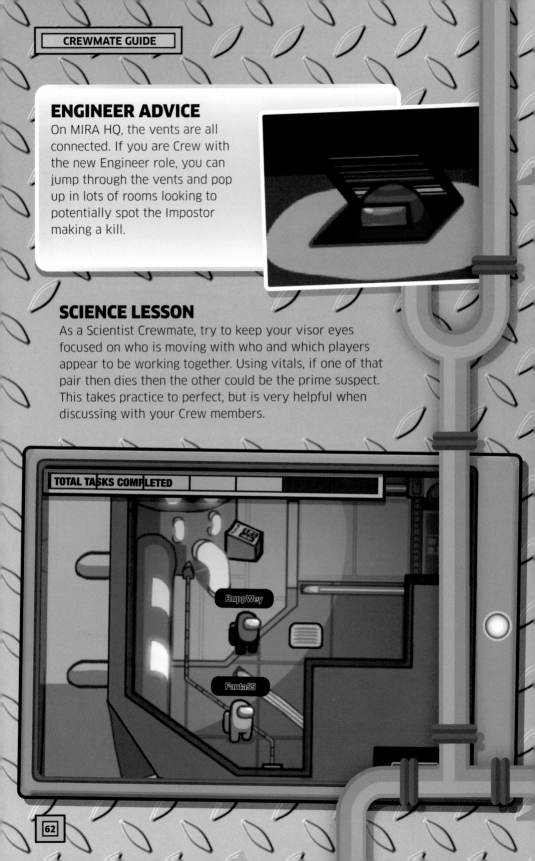

TOTAL TASKS COMPLETED

RuppWey

Fanta55

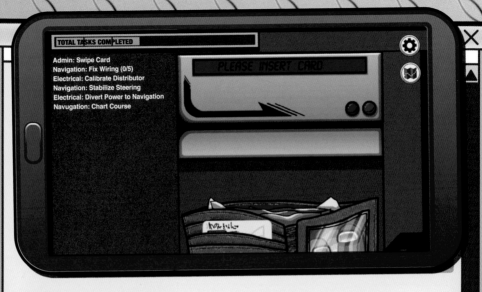

TOTAL TASKS COMPLETED

Admin: Swipe Card
Navigation: Fix Wiring (0/5)
Electrical: Calibrate Distributor
Navigation: Stabilize Steering
Electrical: Divert Power to Navigation
Navugation: Chart Course

PLEASE INSERT CARD

BAR-ILLIANT SPOT

If you clock a player doing a task, then move away from it and the task bar does not rise, then they are not part of your Crew and should be reported. This is not a 100 percent reliable technique, though, as the moment they leave the "fake task", the bar could still rise because of another player finishing a task elsewhere at exactly the same time!

SCREEN SHOCKER

Doing a task that covers most of your screen will make it easier for the Impostor to creep up and kill, as you won't see them.

GOOD TIME

Crew should know how long tasks take to complete. The data task, which is on all maps except MIRA HQ, takes at least eight seconds for the download and the same for upload. Spot a player leaving this task in just two or three seconds, and it could be that they are faking.

My tablet

Headquarters
86%

Estimated Time: 1s

CRITICAL MOVE

If a critical sabotage, such as avert crash course on The Airship, is called, then it is a good idea for one Crewmate to go in the opposite direction and not rush to fix. The Impostor may have called the sabotage to hide a dead body elsewhere on the map.

KILLER TIP

Impostors may be on the lookout for solo players during a critical call, so any move like this is very brave!

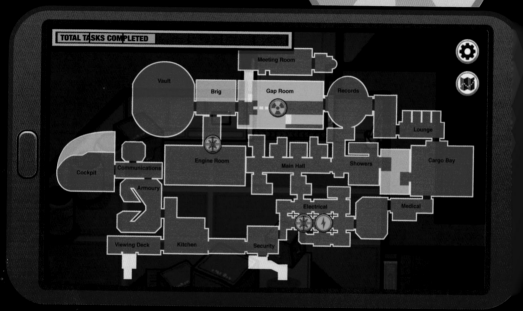

TOTAL TASKS COMPLETED

Vault

Meeting Room

Brig

Gap Room

Records

Lounge

Engine Room

Cockpit

Communications

Main Hall

Showers

Cargo Bay

Armoury

Electrical

Medical

Viewing Deck

Kitchen

Security

VISION FIXED

Fix lights sabotage (all four maps) will scale down the vision of Crew but keep the Impostors' sights just as they were before it was called. Because of this, be suspicious of anyone who appears to be carrying on with their regular activities and isn't struggling in the dark surroundings. Let others know your feelings when you have a meeting.

DeepTrup

MULTI MEMORY

Multi-stage tasks keep players very busy, often moving locations and waiting for timers or cooldowns in order to complete the task in the required order. Fuel engines, upload data, and fix weather node are examples. Catching a player lying about doing these stages in the wrong order should raise the red flag of suspicion.

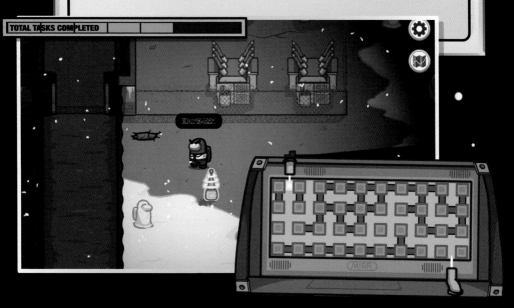

BEWARE THE GAP

The Gap Room on The Airship requires players to use the moving machine to cross the gap. If the equipment is on the wrong side, then you won't be going anywhere and will have to run the long way around. Before you do, if there's a player hovering around that spot and not keen to move on, they could be waiting to use the vent to switch sides. Impostor alert!

QUICK CREWMATE QUIZ

Test your Crewmate survival skills and Impostor-beating knowledge with this speedy quiz.

1
Which one of these is not a genuine Among Us role?
A   Medic
B   Engineer
C   Scientist

2
What did the 2021 update expand the lobby size to?
A   12 players
B   15 players
C   18 players

3
On which map is the Kitchen?
A   The Skeld
B   The Airship
C   MIRA HQ

4
On The Skeld, how many cams can be seen on the screen at the same time?
A   One
B   Six
C   Four

5
In which room must you be to do the clean toilets task?
A   Lounge
B   Locker Room
C   MedBay

6
A sabotage that has potential to end the game is called what?
A   Crucial
B   Critical
C   Essential

7
Crewmates should never need to do what?
A   Lie
B   Communicate
C   Run quickly

8
How many cameras are there in total on MIRA HQ?
A   4
B   8
C   0

Your Answers | 1 | 2 | 3 | 4 | 5 | 6 | 7 | 8 |

IMPOSTOR INSTRUCTIONS

Listen up—stop being Mr. Nice Guy and switch to thinking like an evil hunter! This section schools you on how to become a sneaky and secretive Impostor, with your visor vision set on killing Crewmates to snatch victory. It's not easy, and it needs nerves of steel and ice-cool action, but if you master the role, you'll have Crewmates running scared on every murderous map!

CRUCIAL KILLER MOVES

Understand the basics, and get ready to roam
the map when you're selected as the Impostor.

LONELY BATTLE

You may spawn with one or two other Impostors (three is
the maximum, depending on total Crewmate numbers) but
it's a lonely path playing this role. For victory, you need to
kill enough Crew so there are equal numbers of both, or set a
critical sabotage that the innocent players can't fix in time.

MURDER MOVES

To kill a Crewmate you must
be within close enough range,
depending on the kill distance
configured, so that the kill option
lights up. Tap that and the unlucky
character becomes a pile of bones!
Your next move must be a smart
one. What direction do you run?
Do you vent to escape? Were you
seen on camera? The Crewmate
who discovers the body will call a
meeting to discuss it.

PRACTICE PLAY

Games can be joined with one, two, or three Impostors involved, but the job is awarded randomly. To understand how to be an Impostor, use free play and switch to the role through the Customize option. This isn't the same as in match play, but you can still kill and create sabotages on your map.

BEST BEHAVIOR

Blending in and acting normal are key Impostor skills. Your appearance doesn't give you away, so try to not make your actions do so either. You don't want Crewmates giving you attention early on as a sus player. At some point you will have to kill, vent, and fake tasks, but you'll learn more about these as you read on.

COOLING OFF

Remember what the kill cooldown time is set to by the host. Once you eliminate someone you won't be able to do it again until that time has reset. You'll want to blend your evil enterprises with regular things like fake tasking and moving around the map.

Custom Settings
Map: MIRA HQ
Impostors: 1
Confirm Ejects: On
Emergency Meetings: 3
Anonymous Votes: Off
Emergency Cooldown: 10s
Discussion Time: 15s
Voting Time: 15s
Player Speed: 1.25x
Crewmate Vision: 2.75x
Impostor Vision: 2.75x
Kill Cooldown: 20s
Kill Distance: Short
Task Bar Updates: Never
Visual Tasks: On
Commomn Tasks: 1
Long Tasks: 2
Short Tasks: 5

TRACK TASKS

While you have no ability to move the Crew's task bar level, you should watch for how quickly the tasks fill up. If it nears completion, then defeat will loom and you will have to call some devastating crucial sabotages, or make quick kills to stop a likely loss.

KEEP CALM

This may be easier said than done when you're trying to cover up a dead body, but taking a relaxed and measured approach while you are Impostor is very sensible. Think carefully, don't rush for a kill or harass a Crewmate and make them suspect you. Stay chill, dude!

DEAD BODY REPORTED

SCARY SHAPESHIFTER

When Crew were given the roles of Engineer, Scientist, and Guardian Angel, the Impostor also had an evil new role to hit back with—the power to be a Shapeshifter!

NEW LOOK

If given the Shapeshifter role, you have the Impostor abilities plus the awesome move of morphing into any living Crewmate. Just tap "shift" and choose the Crewmate you want to look exactly like and be seen with the same name as!

Your role is
Shapeshifter

Disguise yourself

LIMITED LOOK

The shift only alters the Impostor's appearance for the time set, but it means the murderer moves undercover and if they vent or kill in view of a Crewmate, that Crewmate will not know their true identity. It's a gamechanger for the Impostor.

KILLER INSTINCT

When dressed like one of the Crew, be brave and kill in front of a witness to get the real owner of the look and the name totally framed in a meeting!

TOTAL TA

Tebbulo

EVIL EVIDENCE

There are drawbacks. Nearby Crewmates will see an animation of the shift happening, and if "evidence" is ticked then when the Impostor switches back to their own suit, evidence will be left on the ground as a clue for the Crew.

TIME OUT

If you have shapeshifted to a Crew look, when a meeting is called you will still appear as regular you. There won't be two identical players sitting in the meeting to give the shapeshifting game away!

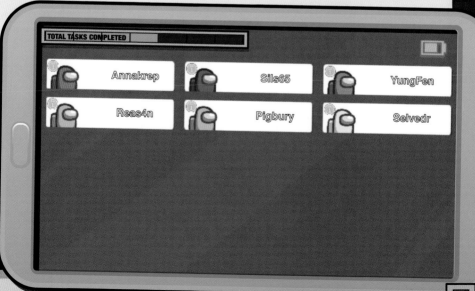

UNDERGROUND AND UNDETECTED

Ducking down vents is something the Impostor will have to do. Here are the strategies around this underground move, and how to make it count.

HIDE OUT

Staying in vents, or "camping," is a popular strategy. You can wait for a player to enter the room, then leap out, kill, and vent away quickly. It's a simple move, but could work once or twice in a game if you pick a good room to hide in.

ENGINEER NOTICE

An Engineer moving through a vent can't be killed by an Impostor at the same time.

UncleDriet

ARROW IN

Once inside a vent, the arrow points you toward where you can travel. There may be more than one arrow, so know exactly where you are moving to. Popping up in a busy area of the map will ramp up the chances of you being seen by the Crew when you reappear, which is not good!

ON STAND-BY

Don't just stand by a vent for a long time, gathering the courage to use it or waiting for others to leave so that you can. It's a big giveaway that you're the killer trying to move around the map in a speedy system.

EXIT & ENTRANCE

If a room has just one entrance, such as MedBay on The Skeld, and you use its vent, try to be aware of who could be just behind you. A Crewmate who saw you enter the room and knows you couldn't have left by a second door, will have you dead to rights if you vent!

FAKE IT TO MAKE IT

Faking tasks is part of the Impostor's game plan. Scan through these tips and tricks on how to fake it to make it through to victory.

TOTAL TASKS COMPLETED

Sabotage and kill everyone.
Fake Tasks:
Admin: Swipe Card
O2: Empty Chute
Navigation: Download Data (0/2)
Reactor: Clean Vent

Tasks

Wirrin

GUIDE LIST

Impostors are handed a list of fake tasks at the start of the match. You can choose to fake these or not—there is no bonus or punishment if you do them or not—but in general, following the list is a good reminder to keep yourself busy and blend in with others.

COMMON GROUND

Never fake a common task. Common tasks include things like fix wiring, enter ID code, insert keys, and swipe card. All Crewmates are given the same common tasks in a match so if, as Impostor, you are seen faking a common that the Crew don't have, then they will know you are sus!

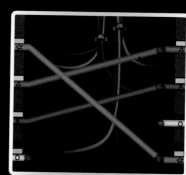

EARLY MOVES

Look busy with your fake tasks quite early in an Among Us match. Crewmates will be doing their tasks early as well, as they want to make the task bar turn green. A player not seen doing tasks, or faking them in your case, will stand out like a sore thumb.

TOTAL TASKS COMPLETED

Admin: Enter Id Code
Balcony: Clear Asteroids (0/20)
Reactor: Divert Power to Communications (0/2)
MedBay: Submit Scan
Reactor: Unlock Manifolds
Office: Process Data

STAND STILL

While you do fake tasks, keep your player very still on screen. If you were doing real tasks, the graphic would appear on your screen and you'd be busy concentrating on that. A player moving a step or two could be a sign of an Impostor not properly focused on trying to fool the Crew.

NoUrSus

SEE SENSE

You've read that doing visual tasks is important for the Crew, as it shows others that they can be trusted. Well, the reverse of this is true for Impostors! Never fake a visual task, as the on-screen action it should trigger will not take place.

ONE MISSION

There is no point in faking a task that none of the Crew can see you do—it's pointless and proves nothing! If a Crewmate enters your room, you need to suddenly look lively and as if you are faking the task like a pro. Job done!

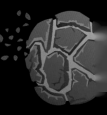

OOD CALL

you are good at particular tasks, enjoy some jobs more
an others, or just have a natural way of doing a few tasks,
en try to always do these first if possible. Chances are
hen you do these as fake, you'll look more believable to
e other players.

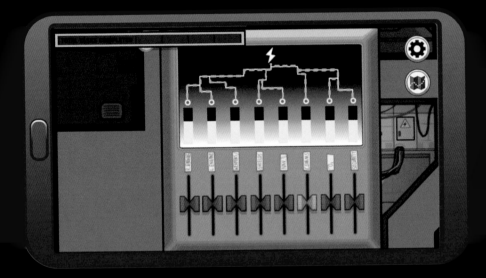

RONG CONNECTION

ost maps have panels and buttons on the wall that do nothing and
on't work with, for example, divert power or fix wiring tasks. Clever
ewmates will know where the non-working panels are, and if you
etend to interact with these, you'll look silly and could get voted out.

SABOTAGE: THE AIRSHIP

This huge Among Us map has plenty of places for Impostors to unleash a scary sabotage!

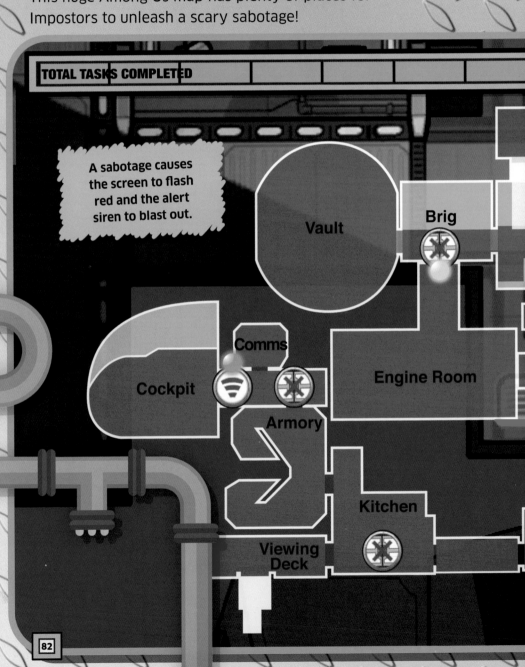

TOTAL TASKS COMPLETED

A sabotage causes the screen to flash red and the alert siren to blast out.

Vault

Brig

Comms

Cockpit

Engine Room

Armory

Kitchen

Viewing Deck

Tap this symbol to sabotage doors and trap Crew in a room.

Avert crash course is a critical sabotage. Tap this and Crewmates have 90 seconds to save their lives!

Quieter areas with less potential for sabotage mayhem. Impostors may seize on this, though, and look to make kills on Crew hiding out.

Causing a communications sabotage stops Crewmates from seeing their list of tasks to do, which doesn't help them achieve their game goal.

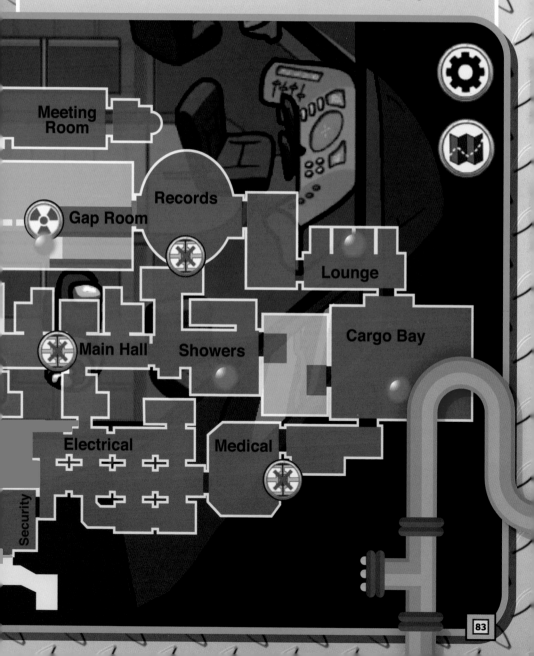

Meeting Room

Records

Gap Room

Lounge

Main Hall

Showers

Cargo Bay

Electrical

Medical

Security

CANCEL COMMS

Comms (communications) sabotage also wipes out the cameras, meaning any Crewmate camped in security watching the screen for signs of the Impostor won't be able to. Comms sabotage is a highly effective trick to play and on a map the size of The Airship, it can split the Crew.

EMERGENCY CREW

All sabotages, apart from door sabotages, wipe out the ability to call an emergency meeting and give the Impostor time to overpower the Crew. There are lots of rooms and corridors to vent to on The Airship, but if you're spotted venting, and you suddenly sabotage, then the Crewmate who saw you won't be able to call a meeting.

SELF FIX

With 15-player lobbies on The Airship, getting suspicious Crewmates off your back can be helped by a quick fix of one of your sabotages. That's right, call a sabotage but then be seen actually helping to fix it! This could fool a Crew or two into thinking you're a good guy.

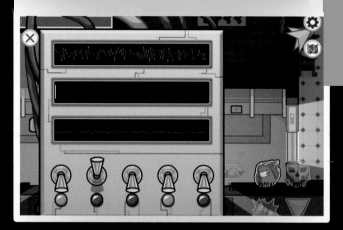

KITCHEN KILLER

The kitchen, in the southwest, is a smart spot to use the door sabotage. If you are inside here with one other lone Crewmate, then lock the doors, make a kill, and escape through the corner vent. There's also no camera to pick you up.

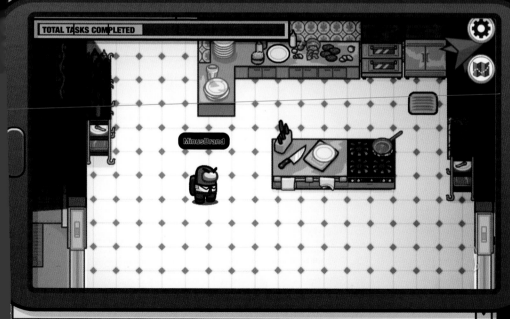

SABOTAGE: THE SKELD

Use the power of your sabotages to cause panic in the Crew, and march to victory on The Skeld!

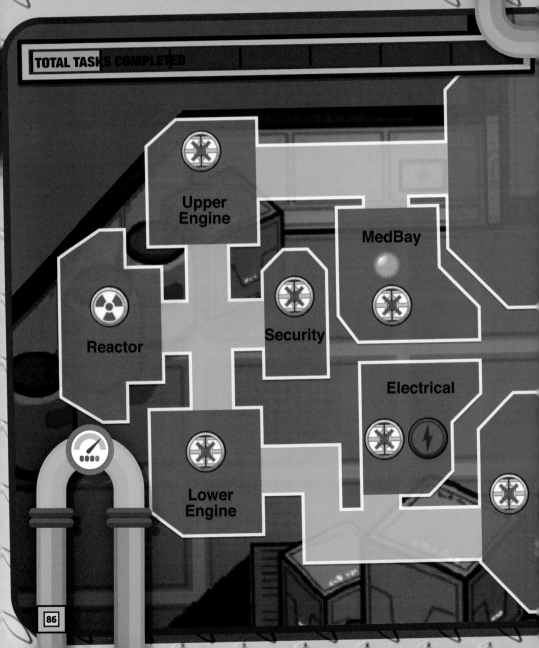

TOTAL TASKS COMPLETED

Upper Engine

MedBay

Reactor

Security

Electrical

Lower Engine

There are four visual tasks on The Skeld: submit scan, empty garbage, clear asteroids, and prime shields.

Reactor meltdown and oxygen depleted are critical sabotages on The Skeld. Fail to fix these and it's game over!

Stay away from visual tasks, like scanning in MedBay, as Impostors can't carry these out and it gives your status away.

Door sabotage is frequently the Impostor's way of forcing Crewmates together and hitting the kill sign before escaping.

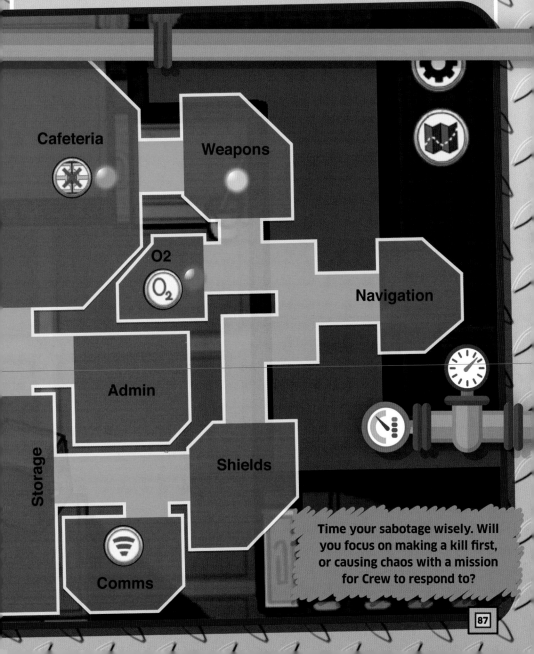

Cafeteria

Weapons

O2

Navigation

Admin

Storage

Shields

Comms

Time your sabotage wisely. Will you focus on making a kill first, or causing chaos with a mission for Crew to respond to?

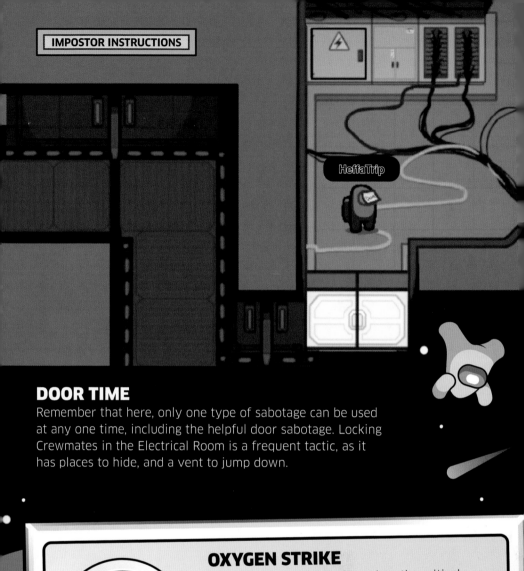

HeffaTrip

DOOR TIME

Remember that here, only one type of sabotage can be used at any one time, including the helpful door sabotage. Locking Crewmates in the Electrical Room is a frequent tactic, as it has places to hide, and a vent to jump down.

OXYGEN STRIKE

Crewmates must move fast when the critical oxygen depleted sabotage is in play! They have just 30 seconds to enter the correct code needed in admin and 02 rooms in the east central area. If an Impostor lurks in the hallway between Lower Engine and Storage or Upper Engine to Cafeteria, this could be a good spot to kill a Crewmate trying to rush to the scene and restore oxygen supplies.

MEGA MELTDOWN

Tap the nuclear hazard sign in the Reactor Room to set off the reactor meltdown sabotage. Another critical danger for Crewmates, it requires two players to press the scanners within just 30 seconds. The Reactor Room, where the two scanners are, is in the far west. Any player remaining in the east, around Navigation and Weapons, is a prime target for an Impostor to kill.

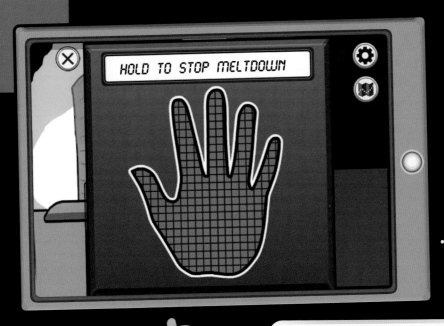

NEWS REPORT

The two critical sabotages on The Skeld are awesome for putting fear into the mind of the Crew, and giving you opportunities to murder. But if a dead body is reported by a Crewmate while the critical sabotage is in action, the emergency meeting it will invoke will bring a stop to the critical mission!

SABOTAGE: MIRA HQ

Sabotaging MIRA HQ requires patience, good timing and knowledge of the limited abilities an Impostor has in this challenging map.

TOTAL TASKS COMPLETED

Sadly, MIRA HQ is the only map that does not have door lock sabotages. There are no lethal lock-ins around this location!

Reactor

Decontamination

Launchpad

There are four ways to sabotage on MIRA HQ. The critical oxygen depleted sabotage is one big move to anger the Crew.

Plunge Crewmates into darkness with the fix lights sabotage. Tap this lightning-like icon to turn off lights.

Sabotaging comms is crucial here. It takes down the door log function which reveals who passes between sensors on the hallway (the upside-down Y between Greenhouse and Cafeteria).

The emergency meeting button is in Cafeteria. Watch for Crew dashing here to call a discussion and rat you out!

- Berggix passed the Southeast sensor
- Berggix passed the Southeast sensor
- Berggix passed the Southeast sensor

LOG OUT

Communications room is in a central location on MIRA HQ, which is tempting for those Crewmates who do want to view the door log readings. Click sabotage comms to wipe this screen and erase any history that you may have dodged the sensors by traveling in the vents.

DOORLOG

`/doorLogMIRA.exe`

[COMMS DISABLED]

DARK TIMES

When the lights sabotage is running, find a secret place to hide and then spring a surprise attack on a fumbling foe on MIRA HQ. The Launchpad has a few good spots and the Office, up in the north, has some great places around the desks and furniture. Stand still and listen for the footprints of Crewmates in the dark.

REACT WELL

Reactor meltdown is not only a critical sabotage that has Crewmates racing to fix it, but the location of the Reactor Room is in the Impostor's favor too. Found in the northwest, the only way to reach Reactor and scan hands to stop the meltdown is through the Decontamination area. An Impostor can lurk in the misty Decontamination zone, make a kill, and then disappear down a vent. It needs quick and precise fingers to make these movements.

WiseFul

122Litten

SABOTAGE: POLUS

Can the Impostor to sabotage their way to victory on Polus?
Find out the options around this large map.

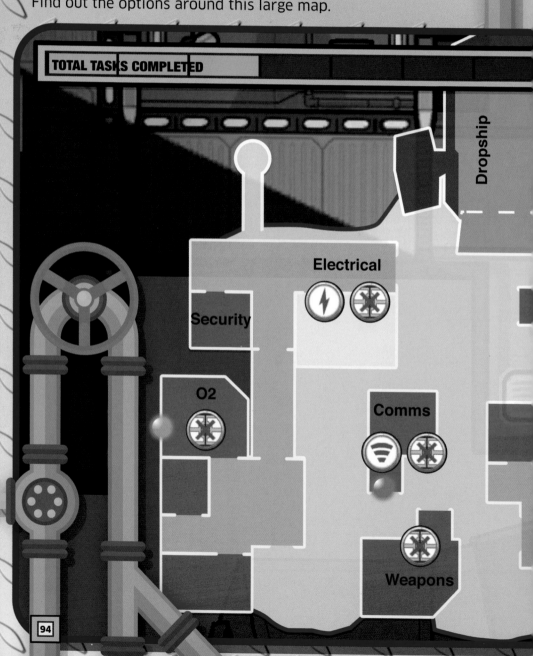

TOTAL TASKS COMPLETED

Dropship

Electrical

Security

O2

Comms

Weapons

Like The Skeld, door sabotage is available here. Storage, near to the dropship spawn point with lots of early-game traffic, is good to lock in and then use the room's vent.

Reset seismic stabilizers is a critical Polus sabotage. It is similar to the reactor meltdown sabotage on The Skeld, and need two handprints from Crewmates.

Make the most of comms sabotaging. It will take down cameras, the vitals monitor, and the admin map.

Polus has an O2 room, but no critical oxygen depleted sabotage. Shame!

Laboratory

Storage

Office

Admin

Specimen Room

UNLOCK OPTION

Although door sabotage is an option, players can quite simply unlock them by configuring the on-screen switch system that applies by each door. With a player's screen taken up with this function, it could give the Impostor a sneaky chance to kill during a simple doors sabotage.

ENTER SPOT

Crewmates rush to the central pylon to a comms sabotage and restore cameras d Impostor monitoring, it may hinder ing able to pick off Crew around the ieter edges of this planetary map. There ll always be brave players, though, who hore the sabotage and carry on doing eir own thing in more remote areas.

DOOR DETAILS

Doors can be closed in Electrical, 02, Laboratory, Weapons, Office, Storage, and Communications. Door sabotage can be used while other sabotages are in play.

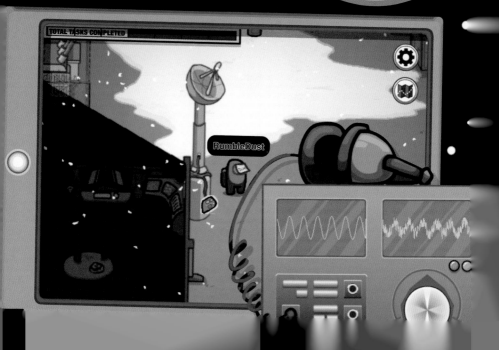

SEISMIC SWITCH

Crewmates have 60 seconds to speed to the two reactors, in the north of the map, to fix the reset seismic stabilizers sabotage before they are defeated. Given the size of the map, this can be tricky to reach in time, especially if players must move up from the south. The reactor to the west of Dropship is quite isolated and ripe for a murderous move!

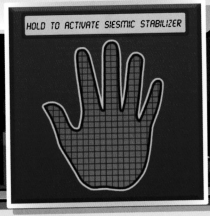

HOLD TO ACTIVATE SIESMIC STABILIZER

LIGHT STRIKE

When the lights sabotage is sprung, will the snowy weather at Polus cause extra panic among the Crew as they race to Electrical to fix it? Maybe this is a good chance for the Impostor to actually step in and fix the sabotage and gather some helpful bonus points and respect in an emergency meeting?

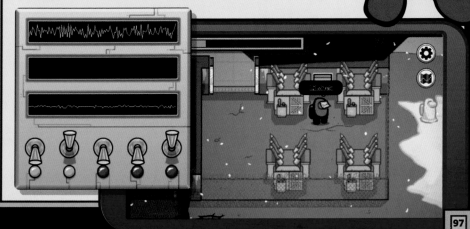

MEETING MISSION

As Impostor, you need to be ready with your replies during deadly discussions in Among Us. Here's how to talk a good game.

FOLLOW ON

If you lack experience in Among Us, don't be too worried about going with the general flow of a meeting. If a couple of Crewmates are hot on blaming someone else, then act calm and follow their lead for a smooth passage to the next round.

SAY SOMETHING

Meetings for Impostors are just as important as they are for when you're working with the Crew. Feelings can run high and the pressure is on as the meeting time counts down. Always have something to say and an opinion, even if you are just asking a simple "who dunnit?" question to the group.

HOLD BACK

When a Crewmate is accused of being the Impostor, don't jump straight in and back up the false claim in a flash. You'll probably come across as too eager to frame that person and get yourself in the clear. Join in, sure, but don't overdo it with your talking.

PRECISE PLAY

Keep your story straight and simple—don't tie yourself up in lies that'll shine through to the group. If you say one thing in a discussion, remember that and don't say something completely different in a following chat. Some Crewmates may remember what you've said.

FRIGHTENING FIGURES

InnerSloth revealed that 37 percent of meetings are called by the emergency meeting button, with 63 percent through dead body reports. Around 95 million meetings are called each day!

'NEER PERFECT

With the introduction of the Engineer Crewmate role, is it a near perfect excuse for the Impostor? If you're brave and bold enough, just claim you are an Engineer during discussion if you are seen going into a vent. It's risky, though, as the genuine Engineer will know you're fibbing!

ZERO TIME

A big plus for the Impostor is when the discussion time is set to zero. This means there's no time for the Crewmates to chat about who the Impostor is, and the vote kicks in right away. When this happens, it means the Impostor blame game is dead in the water and you don't have to cover your tracks with lies!

NEW ORDER

Playing new maps or maps you don't visit very often requires extra prep. Don't slip up during discussions and say the wrong location you were in, or the wrong fake task you were bluffing. Use correct place names and appear confident and powerful in emergency meetings.

WRITE ON

New players may want to quickly write down notes about what they see in a game, ready to report in meetings. As Impostor, this method could be used to jot down which colored suits you think may have seen you vent and could be about to build a case against you in meetings. If you're really rotten, remember who voted against you and seek killing revenge afterward!

LOBBY LISTENING

Players can chat in the pre-game lobby area. At this stage you won't know if you've been selected as Impostor, but looking at this chat could give you a flavor of what your opponents are like and any tactics they may want the group to use. If there's a very vocal player in the lobby, keep a close eye on them during matches.

IMPOSTOR: SNEAKY SKILLS & TIPS

The next six pages are packed with pro tips and tricks to take your Impostor game to an advanced level.

ENGINEER WATCH

Impostors will know who any other Impostors are in their game, so if you spot a player using the vents who is not an Impostor, they must be an Engineer. During discussion, tell the group you saw that player in the vents and press a case for them being an Impostor ... even though you know they're not!

VENT

POLUS PROBLEM

Don't worry about the clean vents Crewmate task on Polus, as it does not apply to this map.

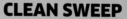

WorryDan

CLEAN SWEEP

Be careful how long you camp inside vents. The short clean vents task, which was added in summer 2021, will flush out any Impostors hiding in the particular vent that's being cleaned by a Crewmate. Camping in vents is sneaky and helpful but can have a downside if a Crewmate uses this task at the right time.

TOTAL TASKS COMPLETED

BE SEEN

Hiding in vents for too long also means you won't be seen very often by Crewmates. You need to be visible and active so that you blend in and don't get unwanted attention or accusations in meetings.

CAMS PLAN

The six cameras on Polus results in there often being a Crewmate sitting in Security watching the screens. Security is isolated up in the far northwest, so burst into the room, make a kill, and then use the vent that's a few steps away outside.

UltrSnag

SHAPE STRATEGY

Shapeshifting allows the Impostor to adopt the appearance of another Crewmate currently on the map. Make sure you do not meet up with the player you have chosen to look like–that person will know their identity has been stolen and others watching on will figure it out too. If you do meet up with your lookalike, try to kill them and make a speedy exit.

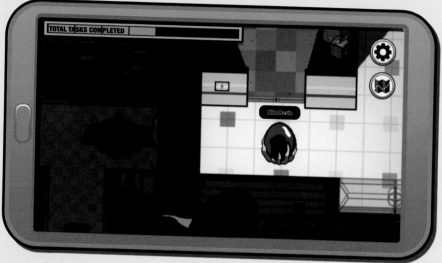

SETTING OUT

Always scan through the game's settings while waiting in the lobby. If Impostor vision is much higher than the Crews' vision, then you have a big bonus. You also need to know how likely it is that the Guardian Angel, Engineer, and Scientist roles will be active in the match.

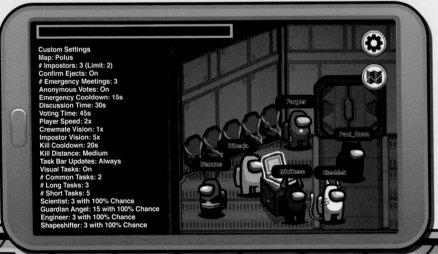

GHOST HELP

Don't forget that as an ejected Impostor, you can still carry on and deploy a sabotage in order to help the living Impostors. Your aim should still be to assist the bad guys in beating the good Crewmates, even though you're out of the game and not visible to living players. As a ghost Impostor, you can sabotage but not use the vents or murder.

DRESS DARK

Some Impostors believe in this tip, but others not so much! Dressing in a black outfit could make you blend in more around the map, especially against dark backdrops, and then be able to sneak up on unsuspecting Crewmates. If this works for you, then great, but dressing in sinister black gear definitely gives an Impostor a dangerous look!

COMMS CHAOS

This shows once again how key the comms sabotage is for Impostors! When triggered by the Impostor, comms being down stops an Engineer from using the vents to chase up the evil players and it also means the Guardian Angel can't use their special protect ability. Don't be afraid to use this a few times during a match that lasts a long time and has a large lobby of players. It will frustrate the Crewmates to the max!

TEAM TACTICS

Impostors should work together during discussions and gang up on a weak or vulnerable Crewmate. If you see an Impostor target a particular Crew member when chatting in a meeting, back your fellow evil player up and try to persuade others to eject that person as well.

STACK ATTACK

This needs nerves of steel, but a stack kill is very impressive and the ultimate Impostor strike. When a group of players are very close together on screen, perhaps doing a task or fixing a sabotage, move among them, wait a second before killing one of them. It could be very difficult for other Crewmates to detect which player made the murderous move!

TOTAL TASKS COMPLETED

Victory

CONTINUE

IMPOSTOR: DEADLY DOS & DON'Ts

Flick through this crucial checklist of things to do and not do as the Impostor. This is your last chance to take in the vital steps you need to take, when you're tasked as the killer.

DO... Be brave enough to murder the Crewmates.

DO... Be active in discussions and chat.

DO... Hit the sabotage button at the right time to unnerve the Crew.

DO... Know your way around each map and where the vents link to.

TOTAL TASKS COMPLETED

Victory

CONTINUE

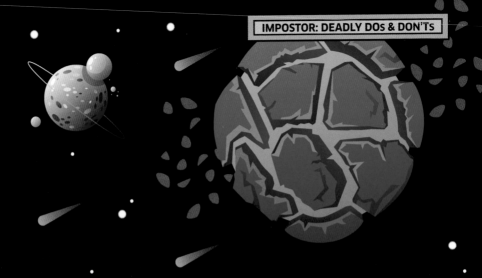

DON'T... Shift or vent in full view of the Crew.

DON'T... Fake visual tasks.

DON'T... Kill where you can be seen by a camera—look for the flashing red light.

DON'T... Call emergency meetings too often as you'll look very sus.

TOTAL TA

Defeat

CONTINUE

INTENSE IMPOSTOR QUIZ

Is your Impostor spacesuit stuffed with stacks of secrets, tips, and fatal facts about how to be a top Among Us killer? Test your skills with these quick-fire questions.

Answers: 1. B; 2. C; 3. A; 4. A; 5. C; 6. B; 7. C; 8. A

1

What is a critical sabotage on The Airship?

A   Divert power
B   Avert crash course
C   Polish ruby

2

What is the minimum kill cooldown time?

A   0 seconds
B   5 seconds
C   10 seconds

3

After shapeshifting, what may be left behind?

A   Evidence
B   Trash
C   A costume

4

What sabotage will pressing the 02 button create?

A   Oxygen depleted
B   Reactor meltdown
C   Communications

5

Where does the vent in the Shields room go to on The Skeld map?

A   Electrical
B   Storage
C   Navigation

6

The proximity setting to murder a Crewmate is known as what?

A   Kill range
B   Kill distance
C   Kill area

7

Which of these will a communications sabotage not have an impact on?

A   Task list
B   Door log
C   Player speed

8

Which map allows you to choose your spawn point?

A   The Airship
B   The Skeld
C   MIRA HQ

Your Answers   1   2   3   4   5   6   7   8

AMONG US NOTES & DETAILS

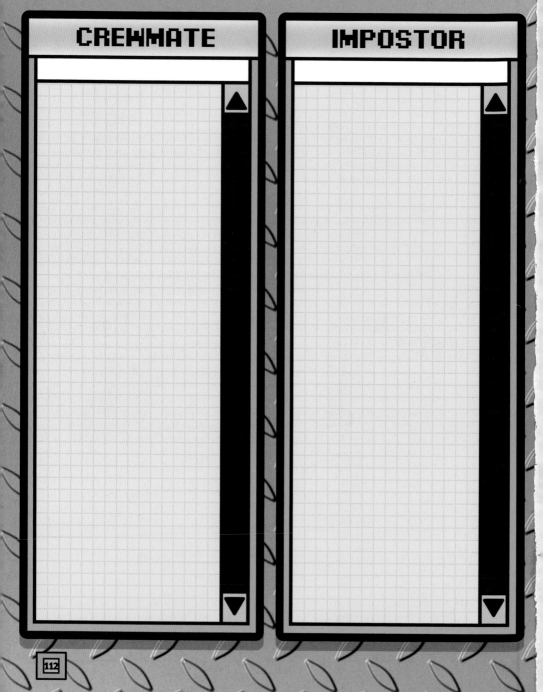

CREWMATE

IMPOSTOR